Mysterious Encounters

Mothman

by Q.L. Pearce

KIDHAVEN PRESS
A part of Gale, Cengage Learning

GALE
CENGAGE Learning

Detroit • New York • San Francisco • New Haven, Conn • Waterville, Maine • London

LIBRARY OF CONGRESS CATALOGING-IN-PUBLICATION DATA

Pearce, Q. L. (Querida Lee)
Mothman / by Q.L. Pearce.
p. cm. -- (Mysterious encounters)
Includes bibliographical references and index.
ISBN 978-0-7377-5037-9 (hardcover)
1. Mothman--Juvenile literature. I. Title.
QL89.2.M68P43 2010
001.944--dc22

2009053703

KidHaven Press
27500 Drake Rd.
Farmington Hills, MI 48331

ISBN-13: 978-0-7377-5037-9
ISBN-10: 0-7377-5037-5

Printed in the United States of America
1 2 3 4 5 6 7 14 13 12 11 10

Printed by Bang Printing, Brainerd, MN, 1st Ptg., 07/2010

Contents

Chapter 1
Two Nights in November   4

Chapter 2
Frightening Encounters   13

Chapter 3
Origins and Sightings   26

Chapter 4
Mothman Today   33

Glossary   41

For Further Exploration   43

Index   45

Picture Credits   48

About the Author   48

Chapter 1

Two Nights in November

The community of Clendenin, West Virginia, is nestled in a land of rolling hills and leafy forests near the banks of the Elk River. On November 12, 1966, the small town became part of a chilling legend. It began as five men were preparing a grave at a local cemetery. A funeral was going to take place the next day so the men were hard at work when a movement in the nearby trees caught their attention. As they watched, a tall winged figure rose into the sky like a giant bird. It flew in a slow circle above the terrified workers before soaring away. Later the men described the creature as humanlike and covered in dark scales. In the days that followed many witnesses reported seeing the creature around the town of

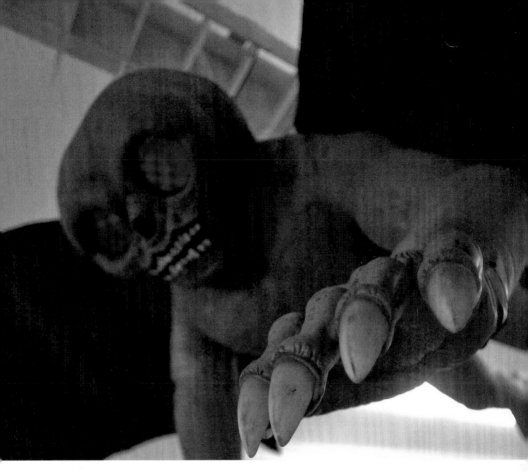

Point Pleasant, West Virginia, has become home to the Mothman, and even has a Mothman museum.

Point Pleasant, 50 miles (80km) away. Since then, the area has come to be known as the home of the bizarre monster known as Mothman.

West Virginia

There had been a few Mothman sightings before 1966, but most people thought the reports were untrue and the stories did not draw much attention. One such tale involved a father and daughter who were traveling on a main highway near the

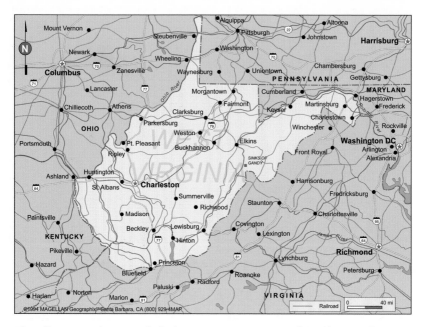

The first Mothman sightings were reported in the early 1960s in West Virginia along the Ohio border.

Ohio River in the early 1960s. The young woman was driving when a tall man stepped into the road. Afraid of hitting him, she jammed on the brakes, but as the car slowed a huge pair of wings unfolded on the man's back and he rocketed into the air. The stories continued to trickle in. In 1965 a woman who lived near the Ohio River told neighbors that her young son had seen an angel in their yard. Soon after, a different woman reported seeing a man who had wings like a huge butterfly. She claimed the creature was at least 6 feet (1.8m) tall.

People finally took notice when two young couples told a fearful tale of what happened to them on the evening of November 15, 1966. Roger and Linda Scarberry and Steve and Mary Mallette had

The TNT Plant

The Mothman chose an interesting place to hide. The West Virginia Ordnance Works (WVOW), also known as the TNT plant, covered more than 8,000 acres (3,237 hectares) on the east bank of the Ohio River. It was made up of large concrete domes that were used to store explosives during World War II. Along with the main factory there were many smaller structures and a network of underground tunnels. The surrounding area of steep ridges and hills was covered in forests.

On the same night that the Scarberrys and Mallettes were chased near Point Pleasant, Newell Partridge was watching television at his home in Salem, nearly 100 miles (160km) away. All at once the screen went blank and an unusual wavy pattern flashed across it. Something outside began to make a high-pitched whining sound and a dog began to howl. Newell grabbed a flashlight and slipped out to see what was making the unusual noise. As he reached the porch the sound stopped. For a moment he could see two glowing red orbs near the hay barn. He later told authorities that they looked like a pair of eyes glaring at him.

been out for a drive near the town of Point Pleasant. Their route took them 7 miles (11.2km) outside of town to an abandoned government facility called the West Virginia **Ordnance** Works. The collection of empty structures was a spooky place at night and young people often went there for fun. As Roger Scarberry drove toward the front gate, he noticed a pair of glowing red lights in the darkness about 7 feet (2m) above the ground. He stopped the car and the four decided to take a closer look. The couples suddenly realized that the red orbs were eyes. Standing in the shadows not far away was a manlike figure with scaly wings wrapped over its back. The four raced to their vehicle. Scarberry slammed the

The small town of Point Pleasant has embraced the Mothman legend.

accelerator to the floor and the car sped down Route 62 at 100 miles per hour (160km per hour). The creature unfurled its wings and lifted into the air. It easily kept pace with the vehicle.

When the car careened into the town of Point Pleasant and pulled up to the Mason County Courthouse, the creature disappeared into the darkness. The frightened young people told their story to Deputy Millard Halstead, who knew and trusted both couples. He believed them and realized that they were truly terrified, but when he followed Roger Scarberry back to the government facility there was no sign of the creature. Later, Scarberry claimed that the monster appeared at his home that night.

The Creature

As the number of sightings grew, word began to spread about the monster of Point Pleasant. It was not long before articles about it appeared in local newspapers. The *Batman* television series was popular at the time, so reporters named the creature Mothman after the character in the series. Although witnesses gave a variety of descriptions, they all agreed that Mothman was about 7 feet (2m) tall with a wingspan of more than 10 feet (3m). It had scaly brown, grey, or dark rust-red skin and big glowing red eyes that some said were on a human-like or insectlike face. Others described the eyes as being embedded in the creature's chest. Some witnesses said the being was completely silent but most agreed that it made a variety of whines, hums, and a terrible screeching sound. It also reportedly caused radio interference and seemed to have mind-control

powers that could fill anyone who saw it with uncontrollable fear. When the creature flew it was able to take off straight up and reach incredible speeds with little effort. The most unusual observation was that Mothman seemed to be drawn to young children but did not want to harm them.

The following night several people gathered in the woods near the TNT plant to search for the strange being that had been reported. They found nothing, but Ralph Thomas and his family were not as fortunate. The Thomas family lived in a **remote** area just outside of Point Pleasant and not far from the WVOW. On November 16th, several members of the Thomas family saw a red light moving in an odd way in the sky above the TNT plant. That evening, Raymond Wamsley, his wife, and Marcella Bennett paid a visit to the Thomas home. Bennett had brought her baby daughter, Kristina. While walking to their car as they were leaving, a tall

Reporters named the mysterious flying creature Mothman because witnesses said it resembled a character from a popular television series.

Two Nights in November **11**

Seeing Is Believing

Many people think that Mothman is nothing more than the product of overactive imaginations. Skeptics point out that the area around the TNT plant is home to many large animals, including big birds such as owls. Light reflecting from headlights or a flashlight may make an animal's eyes appear to glow red. It is possible that the frightened witnesses simply made a mistake.

winged beast with glowing eyes rose up from behind the vehicle as if it had been lying on the ground. When it turned toward them, the horrified visitors ran screaming back to the house. Ralph Thomas pulled them inside, locked the door and turned off all of the lights. Trying not to make a sound, the group huddled together as the creature stepped up onto the porch. It pressed up against the windows trying to see into the darkened room. Wamsley quietly called the police, but by the time the officers arrived, the menacing intruder was gone. Bennett was so frightened by the encounter that she complained of nightmares for months afterward.

Chapter 2

Frightening Encounters

A fter the first flurry of sightings, more people claimed to have encountered the creature throughout the month. On the 18th of November two well-respected local firemen claimed they had seen Mothman in the woods near the TNT plant. Three days later Richard West, a resident of Charleston, called the police. He reported that a huge being with red eyes and wide leathery wings was perched on his neighbor's roof. When the authorities arrived the creature had simply stood, flapped its massive wings, and rose into the night sky. On November 25th, Tom Ury was driving along the same path that the Scarberrys and Mallettes had taken ten days earlier. He saw a remarkably tall, dark

Several of the Mothman sightings occurred in dark wooded areas along the Ohio River. People say they saw a large winged figure with red eyes that flew up into the night sky.

figure standing in a field. It noticed him, too, spread its wings and flew directly over the car before shooting up into the air like a helicopter.

Reports came from many towns along the Ohio River. Ruth Foster of St. Albans frantically called for help when she saw the creature crouching in the yard near her house. On November 27th, Connie Carpenter saw what she believed to be Mothman walking across a deserted golf course near Mason. The creature took to the air and flew toward her car. She reported that she had seen its face clearly and that it was monstrous. Hours later, two young girls were walking past a junkyard in the same area.

The Thunderbird

The Shawnee are a Native American people who have long lived in the area that is now Ohio and West Virginia. Their culture includes stories of an enormous, manlike bird called a Thunderbird. The creature was said to have a wingspan so wide that the flapping of its wings sounded like thunder and caused storms. It was able to emit lightning bolts from its eyes. According to one Shawnee tale, Thunderbirds could take the form of boys and could speak backwards.

They claimed that the creature had suddenly confronted them and chased them. For more than a year the reports continued but they did not always include sightings. Residents found other evidence, such as trails of footprints that ended suddenly as if the being that made them might have flown away. Some people heard loud bumps on the roofs of their homes or strange shrieks in the night. In separate events, five pilots reported that during flights they had seen a red-eyed creature winging its way through the air at amazing speeds. Although some of the details varied, one thing was true of all the sightings: The Mothman often seemed interested in humans, but it never appeared to harm them in any way.

Authors and Journalists

The growing number of tales about Mothman attracted the attention of journalist, author, and researcher John Keel. In December of 1966 he traveled to Point Pleasant to write a story and find out the truth about the creature. At first he was undecided, but as he interviewed witnesses and collected reports, he began to believe the stories were true. He was told tales of lights in the sky, **disembodied** voices, doors that opened and closed by themselves, and cars, televisions, and telephones that suddenly stopped working. At one point he began to receive strange telephone calls from mysterious beings. When the stories started to overlap,

Author and researcher John Keel investigated the mystery surrounding the Mothman and wrote about his findings in a book, *The Mothman Prophecies*.

Keel began to think that the Mothman was part of a larger **conspiracy** that involved unidentified flying objects (UFOs), aliens from other worlds, and even shadowy visitors known as Men in Black. Keel continued his research for months and became an expert on the Mothman. He later published a book about his research called *The Mothman **Prophecies.***

Mary Hyre was another reporter who became involved with the story. She worked for *The Messenger*, an Athens, Ohio, newspaper. Hyre and

Keel became friends. He probably told her about the Men in Black because she reported that she may have been visited by one in January of 1967. Hyre claimed that she had been working late when a short man walked into her office. His appearance was peculiar. His black hair was cut squarely and he wore odd glasses with thick lenses that magnified his strange eyes. In an accent that she did not recognize, the man asked for directions. He stood so close that he made her feel uncomfortable. For most of the time he kept his right hand in his pocket, but before he left he used it to pick up a pen from her desk. He looked at the pen with curiosity as if he had never seen such an object before and took it

Men in Black

The term *Men in Black* (MIB) generally describes mysterious secretive men who show up after unusual events such as UFO sightings. They dress in black suits with thin black ties and dark sunglasses, and they drive unmarked black cars. Those who think the MIB exist believe that these men are agents for unknown private or government organizations. A few think they may be aliens from another world.

with him when he left. Weeks later Hyre saw the man on the street once more. When he saw that she was looking at him he hurried to get into a black car that had pulled up nearby.

The Silver Bridge

About a year after the Mothman sightings in Point Pleasant began, a tragic event took place that made a few think that the creature may have been trying to warn the townspeople about the future. The Silver Bridge was a 700-foot (213m) span that connected Point Pleasant, West Virginia, with Gallipolis, Ohio. On December 13, 1967, two truck drivers said they saw the Mothman perched atop the 40-year-old bridge. They watched until he took flight and sailed away. On December 15th, a single metal connection failed and the bridge collapsed into the Ohio River. It had been packed with rush-hour traffic and dozens of cars sank in the icy water. More than 20 people were rescued but 46 victims drowned. Two bodies were never found.

On the evening of the disaster, members of the James Lilley family, who lived near the TNT plant, reported seeing a dozen odd, moving lights in the sky near their home. They were not the only residents to see the strange lights. A few people later explained that they would have been on the Silver Bridge when it fell if they had not received a mysterious phone call warning them to stay away. One little girl said that the Mothman had appeared at her window the night before the collapse. Strangely, she was not afraid and she felt that the creature did not want to harm

The Silver Bridge connecting Point Pleasant to Gallipolis, Ohio, collapsed in 1967. Some say they saw the Mothman atop the bridge before the collapse and feel that he was trying to warn them.

her. On the day of the accident she and her family piled into their car for a trip. Their route would have taken them over the Silver Bridge. Before they could leave, however, a terrible headache made the girl's father too sick to drive. The girl and her parents believed that Mothman caused the headache to save the child's life.

Many **paranormal** researchers think that Mothmen regularly appear before disasters that will lead to many deaths. Some believe the creatures turn up to warn the victims. John Keel proposed that for a short time the Silver Bridge disaster may have made Point Pleasant a "window" for many types of paranormal activity. Shortly after the accident a second Man in Black was said to have visited Mary Hyre and others. He did not seem to be interested in the bridge collapse but he wanted to know details about UFO sightings in the area. Witnesses described him as dark-skinned with high cheekbones, long fingers, and an odd accent. Mary Hyre gave him some news clippings and he seemed upset that they described aliens as harmful. The man explained that he was a reporter from Cambridge, Ohio, but when questioned he had no knowledge of that area.

Signs of Disaster

West Virginia was not the first place to report Mothman sightings before a **catastrophe** that resulted in a loss of life. Decades before and thousands of miles

One of the more recent sightings of the Mothman was in April 1986 just before the accident at Chernobyl nuclear power plant in the Ukraine.

away in southeastern China, people told stories of a Man-Dragon near the Xiaon Te Dam. The sightings began early in 1926. Frightened villagers described the creature as a large, black-winged man. Many claimed to have seen it circling over the dam. Late in the afternoon of January 19th the huge structure burst, spilling 40 billion gallons of water into the valleys below and drowning 15,000 people. In the late winter of 1947 reports about dark figures and giant red-eyed owls poured into the police station in Texas City, Texas. One month later a cargo ship called the *Grandchamp* that was carrying explosives caught fire in the harbor. The flames quickly spread to other ships and one of them exploded. The blast destroyed much of the town, and all twenty-eight Texas City firefighters were killed. Those who do not believe in the paranormal pointed out that the high number of sightings before the tragedy were just a **coincidence**.

The **outcome** in Freiburg, Germany, in 1978 was much better. When coal miners reported to work on September 10th they found that a giant manlike creature with wide, leathery wings blocked the entrance. Several of the workers thought it might be a **mirage** or someone in a costume. When they tried to approach, the being opened its mouth wide and let out a painful shriek as loud as a siren. As the men huddled together uncertain of what to do next, the ground began to shake. Far beneath them an underground mine shaft exploded and a choking cloud of smoke and flame blasted from the entrance to the mine. When it cleared, the winged figure was gone. No one knew what it was or where it had come from, or even if it had been real. The only thing that was certain was that something had stopped twenty-one miners from entering the mine shaft before the explosion.

One of the more recent reports of Mothman sightings before a major disaster came from Chernobyl, Ukraine, the site of a **nuclear** power plant. In mid-April 1986, several workers at the plant reported seeing a large, winged figure with deep-red eyes. Some claimed that they had received scary telephone calls and others were having dreadful nightmares. On April 26th, an accidental explosion at Chernobyl killed 30 people. The **radioactivity** released by the terrible accident ruined the local environment and led to the deaths of many more people. Some survivors claimed to have seen a huge manlike bird flying in and out of the smoke that rose from the **reactor**. Although witnesses claim otherwise, **skeptics** point out that there is no convincing evidence, such as photographs or videos, proving that Mothman has appeared before any disaster.

Chapter 3

Origins and Sightings

Those who believe that the Mothman or Moth-men exist have many theories about where they may come from and why they appear. Some residents of Point Pleasant propose that the Mothman came to carry out a **curse**. The Cornstalk Curse was placed on Point Pleasant in November 1777. Chief Cornstalk (Hokoleskwa) was a Native American leader of the Shawnee people in the area where a fort once stood and a town exists today. Settlers who lived near the fort had pretended to be friends of the Shawnee, but they betrayed and killed Cornstalk and his son. As he died, the Chief cursed his killers, their descendents, and the land where his blood had been spilled. All that remains of Chief

More earthly explanations for the Mothman's appearance involved mutations in large birds, such as owls.

Cornstalk are three teeth and some pieces of bone, which are sealed inside a stone pillar in Point Pleasant Battlefield State Park. Some people think that the curse also remains and that it was the reason the Mothman arrived. Another **theory** is that Mothman is connected to beings from another world. Several UFOs were reported near Point Pleasant when the Mothman appeared in 1966. Some people believe that the creature itself is an alien life form. This has led a few researchers to think that there may be a link between Mothman and UFOs.

Mothman's appearance may have a more earthly explanation, however. A lot of dangerous explosives and chemicals were once stored at the TNT plant. There is a possibility that over time the chemicals could have caused physical changes, or a **mutation** in large birds such as owls. An even simpler explanation is that the people who reportedly saw Mothman had basically made a mistake. In the 1960s there were many sandhill cranes in the area. They are large birds with red patches on their heads, wingspans of up to 7 feet (2m), and a loud piercing cry. Many of the Mothman sightings were made at night by witnesses who were frightened and

Strange Creatures

Cryptids are creatures that may or may not exist, but have not been scientifically accepted as real. Examples are Bigfoot, werewolves, or sea serpents. Cryptozoology is the study of and search for these beings as well as living examples of animals that are thought to be extinct. Some animals that were once thought to be cryptids but are now known to exist are the okapi and the coelacanth (SEE-luh-kanth).

could have simply mistaken a large bird for Mothman. People who claim to have seen the Mothman disagree, saying the creature looked nothing like a crane.

Mothman around the World

There are reports of Mothmen in countries other than the United States, such as Japan, England, Vietnam, and Mexico. In 1952 at Camp Okubo in Kyoto, Japan, a young soldier was on guard at a military base. Late at night he heard a flapping sound and looked up to see a birdlike creature in the moonlight. The being flew close to the ground and settled not far from the soldier, who became frightened. The young man described the creature as having the body of a man with wings at least 7 feet (2m) across. As it approached him he started to fire his weapon at it, but when he checked the ground after firing he did not find a body. The sound of the firing brought another soldier who reported that a similar sighting had been made a year earlier. In Kent, England, in 1963, four witnesses saw a glowing object streak across the night sky and land in a forested area. At first they thought it might have been a small meteoroid, but they claimed that within moments a dark, manlike figure left the trees and moved toward them. It was headless and had wings like a bat. The witnesses did not wait to see more. In August 1969, in South Vietnam, three American soldiers were sitting on top of a bunker at

Four onlookers in England saw an object flash across the dark sky and land in a wooded area; thinking it was a meteor, they later saw a dark winged figure appear out of the woods.

The Birdman of India

Garuda is an Indian deity that is sometimes compared to Mothman and the Native American Thunderbird. Garuda is shown as having the body of a man and the head and wings of an eagle. He is said to be so huge that the flapping of his wings makes the earth tremble, and he can shoot lightning from his eyes.

night. Something swooped through the sky toward them. Later they all agreed that it was a female creature with batlike wings and black, glowing skin with a greenish tint. The men claimed that she was silent until she started to fly away and they heard the flapping of her giant wings.

The most recent Mothman sighting was in Mexico in the spring of 2009. It took place in La Junta, in the municipality of Guerrero in the state of Chihuahua. The first witness was a student who was returning home on March 6th after a long evening of studying. It was dark, but he noticed something on the road that looked like a person covered with a blanket. All at once the creature stood and flared a giant pair of batlike wings. The frightened young man tried to race away, but the creature chased him. For fifteen minutes it kept pace with his car, staring in the window at him. The student reported that he had been able to get a clear look at it. He described the being as having bloodshot eyes, fur on its face, and a second, smaller pair of wings. After hearing the young man's statement, police searched the area where the creature had appeared, but they found no evidence of it. Even so, other witnesses came forward adding that the being was about 6 feet (1.8m) tall and had hands like those of a kangaroo.

Mothman Today

The story of Mothman has drawn many visitors to Point Pleasant, West Virginia. One thing that most tourists want to do is take a photograph of the amazing Mothman sculpture by Robert Roach. The work was unveiled at a special celebration in 2003. It is a 12-foot-tall (3.6m) statue that stands in Gunn Park in the center of downtown. It is made of stainless steel. The Mothman statue has shimmering red-glass eyes the size of footballs, glimmering wings, and talons on its hands and feet. Surprisingly, the talented sculptor who created the work is not a professionally trained artist. Roach is a retired power company worker.

Because it draws tourists, Mothman has been

The twelve-foot-tall Mothman statue stands in Gunn Park in down-town Point Pleasant, West Virginia.

good for the business community. In order to bring in tourists, the citizens of Point Pleasant honor their famous monster at an annual festival. The first official festival took place in 2002. The activities included exhibits of Mothman-related objects and a hay ride that took visitors to see the sites often mentioned in the stories. In 2005 the Mothman Museum and Research Center opened across the street from the statue. Museum director Jeff Wamsley welcomes visitors daily to see props from a film about Mothman, read historical documents, and view **documentaries** about the creature. The museum also offers tours to the area of the old TNT plant and other sites.

In Print

Fans and believers consider the book *The Mothman Prophecies*, by John A. Keel, a must-read. It was published in 1975 as a work of nonfiction, though skeptics think much of it is made up. Relying on eyewitness accounts, Keel relates the details of the events in Point Pleasant during 1966 and 1967, including the deadly collapse of the Silver Bridge. The author also writes of his theories about UFOs, Men in Black, and even ghosts that might have been linked to the appearance of Mothman. Jeff Wamsley also has written several books about the creature. In 2005 he published *Mothman: Behind the Red Eyes*, which includes recent interviews with several Mothman eyewitnesses, rare documents, press **archives**, illustrations, maps, and photographs.

Mothman in Art and Film

Several artists have paid tribute to the Mothman. Artist Andy Colvin, a native of West Virginia, claims that he has actually seen the creature. Through books, photographs, and film, he has examined the story and expressed how the creature has touched many lives. His art book *The Mothman's Photographer: The Work of an Artist Touched by the Prophecies of the Infamous Mothman* contains nearly 300 photographs of the areas where Mothman was sighted, as well as other related images. According to Colvin's theory, birdmen such as Mothman, Garuda, and Thunderbird are more like superheroes than

In 2002 Richard Gere starred in *The Mothman Prophecies*, which was based on Keel's book of the same name.

Jeepers Creepers

In the 2001 cult classic film *Jeepers Creepers*, a brother and sister on vacation in Florida battle a large-winged being that is similar to Mothman. The creature has batlike wings and takes off straight up when it flies. What makes the film monster different is that it is a predator that stalks and kills its victims.

monsters. He claims that they use messages in dreams and visions to connect with and help ordinary human beings. Many of the photos are drawn from Colvin's reality series of the same name. The series includes interviews with at least fifty eyewitnesses as well as experts such as John Keel.

The 2002 film *The Mothman Prophesies* is a fictional tale based on the book of the same title. Actor Richard Gere plays a journalist much like John Keel. In the movie, the main character is married and his wife is the first to see the Mothman. The story follows the journalist from the death of his wife in a car accident to the collapse of the Silver Bridge. The film was shown in Point Pleasant one day before it was released nationwide. That day the city was mysteriously plagued with phone outages and power blackouts.

Pop Culture

Monsters are often featured in entertainment, including television and video games, and the Mothman is no exception. In 1997 the hit television series *X-Files* aired an episode called "Detour" that included a creature that was similar in some ways to Mothman. The story begins when two workmen are attacked and killed by monsters with glowing red eyes, and local authorities try to track down the killers. The show's two main characters, FBI agents Mulder and Scully, join in the search. Mulder suggests that the creature is related to the Mothman of Point Pleasant. In a 2008 episode of the reality show *Paranormal State*, a team of paranormal researchers travel to Point Pleasant to search for the real Mothman. The group finds no evidence to lead them to believe that the creature exists now or has ever actually visited in the past.

Mothman has become a character in several cartoons, too. In the animated Cartoon Network series *Aqua Teen Hunger Force*, Mothmonsterman appears in the episode "The Bus of the Undead." *Aqua Teen Hunger Force* is about the adventures of three fast-food items—fries, a milkshake, and a burger—that can morph into other forms such as a hotdog. Their archenemy, Dr. Weird, creates the moth/human Mothmonsterman, who attacks the Hunger Force. The main villain in the Nickelodeon TV series *Invader Zim*, is an alien from planet Irk

An episode from the television series *The X Files* centered around a Mothman-like creature.

who plans to destroy the Earth. One of the only humans who is aware of the plot is a boy named Dib, codename Mothman. The hit cartoon *Sponge-Bob SquarePants* also appears on Nickelodeon. In the episode "Night Light," Mothman is one of Mermaid Man's archenemies.

Through books, movies, and television, Mothman has become known around the globe and sightings are still being reported. But what really happened in Point Pleasant four decades ago? Did

Playing Games

The Mothmen have also been a popular element of several role-playing games such as _Shin Megami Tensei III: Nocturne_ for the Playstation 2 game system. In _Castlevania: Dawn of Sorrow_ and _Portrait of Ruin_ for Nintendo DS, Mothman is a hidden monster.

Mothman come to deliver a warning, or were the sightings and the disaster at Silver Bridge unrelated? Did the creature really appear to dozens of startled eyewitnesses, or were those who reported seeing him the victims of overactive imaginations? It is unlikely that the early reports were a hoax because many of the witnesses were respected members of the community. It is possible that they were simply mistaken or merely caught up in the excitement over strange events that seemed to grip the small town. There is no doubt that the area experienced a flurry of reports about a winged creature, odd lights in the sky, televisions and telephones that suddenly stopped working, mysterious Men in Black, and more. But if Mothman did visit Point Pleasant, as many people believe, he left behind more questions than answers.

Glossary

archive: A collection of documents, such as letters and photographs, that are of historical interest.

catastrophe: A disastrous event that may lead to loss of life.

coelacanth: A rare living prehistoric fish that was once thought to be extinct.

coincidence: Events that seem to be connected but actually happened by chance.

conspiracy: An agreement between two or more people to commit an act that is improper or illegal.

curse: A supernatural wish to bring harm to someone else.

deity: A being that is considered holy or divine.

disembodied: A voice or presence with no physical form.

documentary: A factual film or television show about a particular topic.

extinct: Having ceased to exist.

mirage: An illusion that may be a trick of light or imagined.

mutation: A random change or variation in a life form.

nuclear: Relating to atomic energy.

okapi: An African mammal that looks like a cross between a giraffe and a zebra.

ordnance: Military weapons and supplies.

outcome: The final result of a series of events.

paranormal: Something that exists outside of the expected that cannot be explained scientifically.

predator: An animal that hunts and eats other animals.

prophecies: Predictions of future events.

radioactivity: High-energy particles released by certain materials.

reactor: A device in which a nuclear reaction takes place.

skeptic: Someone who expresses doubts about a topic or questions a result.

theory: A set of facts and that leads to an idea of how something happened or how it works.

For Further Exploration

Books

Janet Corimer, *Strange but True Stories—Book 2: Bob Lazar, the UFO Guy/ the Mothman Mystery/ Mischievous Spirits ... and More.* Irvine, CA: Saddleback, 2006. A collection of stories about unusual creatures and legends. Most are based on eyewitness accounts. The book includes a teacher resource guide.

Kelly Milner Halls, Rick Spears, and Roxyanne Young, *Tales of the Cryptids: Mysterious Creatures That May or May Not Exist.* Plain City, OH: Darby Creek, 2006. A fun and thorough overview of cryptozoology and a host of wonderfully weird creatures. It includes illustrations, photographs, and a reality index to help readers make up their own minds.

Lisa Wade McCormick, *Mothman: The Unsolved Mystery.* Mankato, MN: Capstone, 2009. A complete overview of Mothman and the events in Point Pleasant in the 1960s, as well as information about how science is trying to solve the mystery.

Karen Miller, *Monsters and Water Beasts: Creatures of Fact or Fiction?* New York: Henry Holt, 2007.

An overview of many legendary creatures, such as Mothman. The book includes interviews with witnesses and scientists.

Web Sites

The Cryptid Zoo (www.newanimal.org). A very thorough site about cryptozoology. Dozens of cryptids are listed alphabetically.

Mothman Lives (www.mothmanlives.com). This is the official Mothman Museum site. It includes photos, up-to-date sightings, information on Point Pleasant, viewer art, and more.

Mothmen.U.S. (www.mothmen.us). An excellent site with stories, sightings, photos, videos, and links.

WestVA.net (www.westva.net/mothman). Links to fourteen original 1966 articles about the Mothman sightings.

Index

Animals, extinct, 28
Aqua Teen Hunger Force (cartoon series), 38
Art, Mothman in, 36

Batman, 9, *10–11*
Bennett, Kristina, 11, 12
Bennett, Marcella, 11
Bigfoot, 28
Birdman of India, 31, 36

Camp Okubo (Kyoto, Japan), Mothman sighting in, 29
Carpenter, Connie, Mothman sighting by, 16–17
Cartoon Nework series *Aqua Teen Hunger Force,* 38
Castlevania: Dawn of Sorrow and Portrait if Ruin (Nintendo DS game), 40
Chernobyl nuclear power plant accident, Mothman sighting prior to, *23,* 25
Clendenin, West Virginia, Mothman sightings in, 4
Coelacanth, 28
Colvin, Andy, 36, 37
Cornstalk, Chief (Hokoleskwa), 26–27
Cryptids, 28
Cryptozoology, 28
Curse, as origin of Mothman, 26

"Detour" (*X-Files*) 38, 39

Dib, 39
Disaster, Mothman sightings as sign of, 20–25, *23*

Elk River, 4
Extinct animals, 28

Film, Mothman in, 36–37
Foster, Ruth, Mothman sighting by, 16
Freiburg, Germany, coal mine explosion in, 24–25

Gallipolis, Ohio, collapse of Silver Bridge near, *20–21,* 21–22, 35, 40
Garuda, 31, 36
Gere, Richard, *36,* 37
Grandchamp (cargo ship), 24
Gunn Park, Mothman sculpture in, 33, *34*

Halstead, Millard, 9
Hokoleskwa, 26–27
Humans, Mothman interest in, 17
Hyre, Mary, research into Mothman, 18–20, 22

India, birdman of, 31
Invader Zim (Nickelodeon), 38–39
Irk (planet), 38–39

Jeepers Creepers (film), 37

Keel, John, *18*, 35, 37
  research into Mothman, 17–18,
    20
Kent, England, Mothman sighting
  in, 29, 30
Kyoto, Japan, Mothman sighting
  in Camp Okubo in, 29

La Junta, Mexico, Mothman sighting in, 31–32
Lilley, James, family, Mothman
  sighting by, 21–22

Mallette, Mary, Mothman sighting
  by, 6, 7, 8–9, 13
Mallette, Steve, Mothman sighting
  by, 6, 7, 8–9, 13
Man-Dragon, sighting of, near
  Xiaon Te Dam, 23–24
Mason, West Virginia, 16
Mason County Courthouse, 9
Men in Black (MIB), 18, 19, 22,
  40
Mermaid Man, 39
The Messenger (Athens, Ohio,
  newspaper), 18
Mirage, 24
Mothman
  annual festival honoring, 35
  around the world, 29, 31–32
  in art and film, *36*, 36–37
  books on, 35–36
  curse as origin of, 26
  description of, 4, 6, 7, 9–12,
    19–20, 28–29, 31–32
  documentaries about, 35
  eyes of, 7, 8, 10, 12, 32
  flight of, 4, 6, 9, 11, 13, 16
  interests in humans, 17
  investigation into, 17–20, 22
  mind-control powers of, 10–11
  movement of, 11
  naming of, 9
  in pop culture, 38–40
  radio interference and, 10

sculpture of, 33, *34,* 35
sightings of
  along Ohio River, *14–15*
  by Bennett, Marcella, 11–12
  by Carpenter, Connie, 16–17
  in Chernobyl, Ukraine, *23,* 25
  in Clendenin, West Virginia, 4
  by Foster, Ruth, 16
  in Freiburg, Germany coal
    mine disaster, 24–25
  in Kent, England, 29, *30*
  in La Junta, Mexico, 31–32
  by Lilley, James, family, 21–22
  by Partridge, Newell, 7
  in Point Pleasant, West Vir-
    ginia, 5, *5,* 27, 39–40
  by Scarberrys and Mallettes, 6,
    7, 8–9, 13
  as sign of disaster, 22–25
  at Silver Bridge collapse, *20–21,*
    21–22, 35, 40
  in South Vietnam, 29, 31
  in Texas City, Texas, 24
  by Thomas, Ralph, 11, 12
  by Ury, Tom, 13, 16
  by Warmsley, Raymond, 11–12
  by West, Richard, 13
sounds made by, 7, 10, 24, 28
theories on, 27, 29, 37
wings of, 4, 6, 8–9, 29, 31–32
Mothman: Behind the Red Eyes
  (Wamsley), 35–36
Mothman Museum and Research
  Center, 35
The Mothman Prophecies (film),
  36, 37
The Mothman Prophecies (Keel),
  18, 35
*The Mothman's Photographer: The
  Work of an Artist Touched by the
  Prophecies of the Infamous Mothman* (Colvin), 37
Mothmonsterman, 38

Nickelodeon
  Invader Zim, 38–39
  "Night Light," 39

Ohio River, 6, 7
  collapse of Silver Bridge into,
    20–21, 20–22, 35, 40
  Mothman sightings along, 14–15
Okapi, 28
Owls, 12, *27*
  mutations in, 27, 28

Paranormal research, 22
Paranomal State (reality show), 38
Partridge, Newell, Mothman sight-
  ing by, 7
Point Pleasant, West Virginia, 8–9,
  17, 26
  annual festival honoring Moth-
    man in, 35
  collapse of Silver Bridge near,
    20–21, 20–22, 35, 40
  Mothman sculpture at, 33, *34,*
    35
  Mothman sightings in, 5, *5,* 27,
    39–40
Point Pleasant Battlefield State
  Park, 27
Pop culture, Mothman in, 38–40

Radioactivity, 25
Radio interference, 10
Roach, Robert, Mothman sculp-
  ture by, 33, *34,* 35

St. Albans, 16
Salem, West Virginia, 5
Sandhill cranes, 28
Scarberry, Linda, Mothman sight-
  ing by, 6, 7, 8–9, 13
Scarberry, Roger, Mothman sight-
  ing by, 6, 7, 8–9, 13
Sea serpents, 28
Shawnee people, 16, 26–27
  Thunderbird legend of, 16

Shin Megami Tensei III: Nocturne
  (Playstation 2 game), 40
Silver Bridge, 20–21
  collapse of, *20–21,* 21–22, 35, 40
Skepticism, 12, 25
South Vietnam, Mothman sighting
  in, 29, 31
SpongeBob SquarePants (cartoon),
  39

Texas City, Texas, Mothman sighting in, 24
Thomas, Ralph, Mothman sighting by, 11, 12
Thunderbird, 31, 37
  legend of, 16
TNT plant, Mothman sightings
  near, 7, 11, 13, 21, 35

Unidentified flying objects
  (UFOs), 18, 22, 27, 35
Ury, Tom, Mothman sighting by,
  13, 16

Wamsley, Jeff, 35
Wamsley, Raymond, 11, 12
Werewolves, 28
West, Richard, Mothman sighting
  by, 13
West Virginia
  Mothman sightings in, 5–6, *6,*
    8–9
  Mothman sightings in Clen-
    denin, 4
  Mothman sightings in Point
    Pleasant, 5, 27, 39–40
West Virginia Ordnance Works
  (WVOW), 7, 8
World, Mothman sightings around
  the, 29, 31–32

X-Files "Detour," 38, *39*
Xiaon Te Dam, sighting of Man-
  Dragon near, 23–24

Picture Credits

About the Author

Q. L. Pearce has written more than 100 trade books for children, and more than 30 classroom workbooks and teacher manuals on the topics of reading, science, math, and values. Pearce has written science-related articles for magazines; regularly gives presentations at schools, bookstores, and libraries; and is a frequent contributor to the educational program of the Los Angeles County Fair. She is an assistant regional adviser for the Society of Children's Book Writers and Illustrators.